HOW TO BE A CELEBRITY

by Mifflin Lowe

PRICE STERN SLOAN
Los Angeles

Published by
Price Stern Sloan, Inc.
360 North La Cienega Boulevard
Los Angeles, CA 90048

ISBN 0-8431-2434-2

10 9 8 7 6 5 4 3 2 1

First Printing

TABLE OF CONTENTS

PART II: THE BIZ

PART III: THE LIFE

"Fame is a food that dead men eat."

Henry Austin Dobson

"There's a sucker born every minute."

Phineas Taylor Barnum

FOREWORD

In 1986 I wrote a book called THE CHEAPSKATE'S HANDBOOK. Thanks to a relentless publicity agent, I was thrust into the limelight. Suddenly, I was doing interviews on national TV. Suddenly, my parents were able to talk about me in public without feeling a deep sense of shame and regret. My God, my book was even translated into Italian and Swedish, languages from which I'd previously known two words: "linguini" and "fjord."

Then I realized that if I could do it, anybody could do it. All it takes is chutzpah, a little show biz savvy and a willingness not to get out of the way if anybody from a TV station points a camera in your direction. In fact, if Andy Warhol was right, each of us will be famous for at least fifteen minutes. The trouble is nobody's doing anything to prepare us. And that's what this book is all about. So read, learn, enjoy and start getting ready for your moment in the sun. If Andy was right, it won't last long, so pay close attention.

Your close, personal friend,
Mifflin Lowe

CELEBRITIES: A BRIEF HISTORY

In the old days, with the exception of an infrequent religious figure, most celebrities were people like Alexander the Great, Genghis Khan and Charlemagne, i.e., people who were likely to kill you—and everybody you knew—and were thus difficult to ignore. In short, celebrities were people who did something of great historical import *first* and then became famous later. So it continued for thousands of years until the invention of the printing press, the radio and the *Bob Hope Christmas Special*. Today, things are more or less the other way around. First, people become celebrities—football players, actors, what-have-you—and *then* they're elected to high office and entrusted with the fate of nations and lives of billions. It just shows you how far we've come.

CELEBRITY APTITUDE TEST

With the exception of a few farmers and guys who want to grow up to be forest rangers, there are probably only ten or twelve people in the world who don't have the desire and ability to become celebrities of one sort or another. Thus the real objective of this test is not so much to discover whether you have the right stuff to become a celebrity, but rather to figure out what route to take.

1. Who's the most important person in the world?
   (a) the President
   (b) the Pope
   (c) Bert Parks

2. If you could have anything you wanted this year for Christmas, what would you wish for?
   (a) peace on earth
   (b) an end to world hunger
   (c) a guest appearance on an Oprah Winfrey special

3. What's the most beautiful thing you've ever seen in your life?
   (a) a sunset
   (b) the Sistine Chapel
   (c) a mirror

4. How do you usually think of yourself?
   (a) as a nice person
   (b) as an average person
   (c) in the third person

5. What would you do if you saw somebody peeking at you through a window?
   - (a) pull down the shade and leave the room
   - (b) call the police
   - (c) take off your clothes and dance around

6. The center of the solar system is
   - (a) the sun.
   - (b) the earth.
   - (c) somewhere in Beverly Hills.

7. When you were a child, what did you want to grow up to be?
   - (a) a doctor
   - (b) a college professor
   - (c) Monty Hall

8. What's your favorite inspirational song?
   - (a) the national anthem
   - (b) "Rock of Ages"
   - (c) "My Way"

9. If you could be anybody in world history, who would it be?
   - (a) Albert Einstein
   - (b) Albert Schweitzer
   - (c) Alan Alda

10. If a movie you'd starred in became a box office smash, how would you feel?
    - (a) deliriously happy
    - (b) grateful to your fans
    - (c) you'd still rather direct

11. What is the lowest form of life?
   (a) the amoeba
   (b) the single cell slime mold
   (c) the critic

How To Score

Give yourself ten points for each "c" answer, five points for each "b" answer and zip for every "a" answer.

100+	Star of screen
90-99	Star of stage
80-89	Talk show host
70-79	Game show host
60-69	Bert Parks
50-59	News anchorperson
40-49	Fitness advisor to the stars
30-39	Donald Trump
20-29	PBS celeb
10-19	Celebrity dentist
0-9	Forest ranger

CELEBRITY HOMEWORK: Who would you rather be, Albert Einstein or Alan Alda? Tell why in twenty-five words or less.

Part I

THE OPPORTUNITIES

So, What Do You Want To Be When You Grow Up?

How To Be A
Celebrity Actor:
The Method

Most people who want to be celebrities choose to become actors since it involves a lot less work than almost anything else and, besides, it's almost impossible to prove that anyone is not an actor—especially in the movies, where you can always do a second take.

Other than the fact that you must constantly remind people you are one, here's all you have to remember to establish yourself as a legitimate thespian.

1. If you're a comedian, say you're ready for a serious role.

2. If you usually play serious roles, say you'd like to try your hand at some comedy for a change.

3. In either case, acting is your craft.

4. Your body is your instrument.

5. You'd rather direct.

As an actor, you will have an important decision to make at the inception of your career. Should you go to New York and become a skilled professional? Or should you go to Los Angeles? If you go to New York, expect to wait on tables for the rest of your life and spend most of what you earn taking lessons at the Actors' Studio. If you go to L.A. you may have to bus tables at Bob's Big Boy for a week or two, but soon you'll have steady work as a TV cop and be on your way to megastardom. Best of all, you'll never have to take an acting lesson in your life, so you can save your tips and spend them on something you really need, like a nose job.

Also remember, if you go to New York, you must insist on doing summer stock long past the point where it makes any economic sense because of your "deep and abiding love affair" with the theater; whereas, in Los Angeles, you will be required to have a deep and abiding love affair with nothing other than yourself.

CELEBRITY HOMEWORK: Get together with a friend and practice doing interviews. Ask, "What was it like working with Dustin Hoffman?" "Where do you go from here?" and stuff like that. End your "interview" by saying, "This is the best work I've ever done."

Where An Actor Goes To Forget: The Soaps

As a soap opera celeb, you will play roles that would best be handled with rubber gloves, and will be worshipped by people whose next favorite thing in life is feeding poisoned popcorn to pigeons. Nonetheless, you'll get to appear at supermarket and shopping mall openings all across the country where you'll be mobbed by adoring fans. (The only drawback, of course, is that most of your fans will give every indication that a mob is their natural environment.) At any rate, the work is steady and the only thing you have to remember is that you don't remember anything. To determine if you have the aptitude for this kind of work, simply respond to the following questions.

1. What is your name?

2. Where are you from?

3. Where have you been for the past year-and-a-half?

If your answer to any of these questions was "Who," "Huh" or "What," you may well have precisely the quality directors of soap operas are looking for: amnesia.

CELEBRITY HOMEWORK: Get together with your parents, siblings and old friends for the weekend. Pretend you've never seen them before.

Turkeys In The Straw: Country and Western Stars

Folks expect a country and western celebrity to be humble and honest, so remember, no matter how arrogant and unbearable you are in real life, as soon as you step on stage or in front of a TV camera, you've gotta get down—to earth, that is. And don't worry about how well you can sing or play—let's remember, spoons are considered instruments in C&W music—what's important is establishing that you have the right background and the proper breeding.

1. YER DADDY. It doesn't matter whether your father was an equities analyst or an investment banker specializing in conglomerate mergers, if you want to be taken seriously as a C&W celeb, you must always insist your dad was one of the following:
   a. a coal miner
   b. a share cropper
   c. a truck driving man

2. MAMA TRIED. Your mother, of course, was a good woman who worked a minimum of nineteen hours a day and gave issue to a litter of at least seventeen children, none of whom had shoes or anything much to eat before the age of five. Your mother probably died in childbirth. If

she didn't, it's not because she wasn't trying.

3. YOU ON THE OTHER HAND. If male, you used to be a hard-drinking, pill-popping, womanizing, no 'count S.O.B., who was jailed on a regular basis for all the above forms of behavior but now loves Jesus. If female, you were married by age twelve to a male who fits the preceding description.

4. DRESS FUNNY. As a C&W celebrity you will be expected to lack sophistication in all forms of advanced social behavior and particularly in sartorial matters. In short, you'll have to dress like a clown. When appearing in public, men should look like a cross between Elvis Presley and Davy Crockett; women should dress as though on their way to a Halloween square dance. In either case, any ensemble, including underwear and pajamas, with fewer than thirty rhinestones per square inch is probably not correct.

5. TALK FUNNY. As a C&W celeb, your fans will take great delight in hearing you say things like, "I swear, you look like you been rode hard and put up wet." Even if you're from Bayonne, you should sound as though freshly plucked from a cotton field or coal

mine, and whenever possible, you should spice interviews and public appearances with colorful colloquialisms.

COLORFUL COUNTRY AND WESTERN EXPRESSIONS

1. shucks
2. shoot
3. git
4. funnin'
5. Kinfolks
6. y'all
7. hombre*
8. roots
9. ruckus
10. cotton (as a verb)

WORDS TO AVOID

1. angst
2. raison d'être

---

* *Use "hombre" judiciously and only in conjunction with the word "tough." Overuse of the word could tend to lead to a widespread belief you're a member of a salsa band.*

3.   stock options*

CELEBRITY HOMEWORK: Write a song about your dad, dog or truck. Use a minimum of eight of the above colorful expressions.

*   *If used in reference to cattle, this term is acceptable.*

As a C&W celeb, you'll be expected to dress
as funny as you talk.

Pardise On Earth:
Religious Celebrities

Not even Redford is bigger than a genuine religious celebrity. Sadly, it's not as easy to become identified as a "True Prophet" or the "Offspring of God" as it once was, but that doesn't mean there's not still plenty of opportunity. Even if you don't become the Pope, with the proliferation of cable channels, it's still relatively simple to become a TV evangelist with power, perks and some rather spectacular tax breaks.

If you have ever considered becoming a TV evangelist, there are two questions you must ask yourself and answer honestly to determine if you have the necessary "spiritual" qualities.

1. You think of money as
   (a) the root of all evil.
   (b) what I want.

2. The only thing God cannot forgive is
   (a) murder.
   (b) bad ratings.

If you answered "b" to both questions, you've got the right stuff. Now all you need is (a) a Bible (b) a polyester suit and (c) a friend who heals on command.

Incidentally, many people are delighted to discover that these days you don't even have to deny yourself any of life's pleasures to be a religious celeb. And if you ever do get caught with your fingers in the till, or your hands on someone else's wife, all you have to do is go on TV, shed a few tears and people will start to send money again.

CELEBRITY HOMEWORK: Ask a friend for money. If he gives you some, ask for more.

TV Evangelism. Good work if you can get it,
and you can get it if you cry.

Bigger Is Better: Opera Celebs

This is probably not a wise choice, given the fact that you'll have to undergo years of training and still end up with a voice that will annoy ninety-nine out of one hundred people. However, the perks can be great. Greek shipping magnates of Croesian wealth seem to find opera stars ferociously attractive, which means you can expect to spend summers on a yacht, evenings at glitzy parties and most of the rest of the time wolfing down cheese blintzes in expensive restaurants, which is okay since opera is one of the few performing arts outside of professional wrestling in which nobody seems to care how fat you get. Another plus is that opera celebs are not just allowed to be but, indeed, expected to be, vain, irritating and temperamental. In fact, if you don't throw a plate of pasta at someone every once in a while, people will just assume you can't sing anymore. However, there are risks. If you don't become a star of the first magnitude, you will spend the rest of your life carrying a spear while singing background choruses in a language most of the audience won't understand, and not even your mother will consider you a success.

CELEBRITY HOMEWORK: Go to a 24-hour, all-you-can-eat restaurant. Don't leave until you're ejected by the management.

Less Is More: Celebrities In The Ballet

Like sports, the ballet requires hard training, dedication and raw athletic ability, which means that from the time you're six years old until you're too old to do it anymore, you'll have to spend most of your free time in a smelly room doing deep knee bends next to someone whose tights desperately need to be washed. Realistically, unless you find yourself in a position to defect from a communist country, you may as well forget it anyway. At most, you'll get a chance to wave your arms around in a corps de ballet pretending you're a swan, and sooner or later you'll suffer from obscure pains, as well as painful obscurity. Worse yet, you won't get to eat a decent meal until you retire; and if you're male, everyone will know the exact size and shape of your pudenda. All in all, forget becoming a ballet celeb, unless you're in it strictly for the masochism. However, if you have an irrepressible urge to wear skimpy outfits and run about in front of people leaping through the air, you may wish to consider a more lucrative way to pursue this activity: basketball.

CELEBRITY HOMEWORK: Put on tight underwear and give yourself a "wedgie." Walk through the living room in front of guests.

It's Not Whether You Win Or Lose: Game Show Celebrities

A particularly American art form, the game show is the place we may study celebrityhood in its most pure form, unadulterated by any pretensions to talent beyond the simple ability to read one and two syllable words from an idiot card. If you want to become famous in a hurry, the game show presents three intriguing possibilities.

THE HOST

Being the host is, unquestionably, the easiest way to be a celebrity on a game show and doesn't merit protracted discusssion. In truth, you could instantly transform almost any vacuum cleaner salesman in the world into a passable game show host with little more than the following:

1. contact lenses

2. a clean toupeé

3. a girdle

Other than these, a prospective game show host needs only the capacity to walk across a smooth linoleum floor without tripping on his own microphone wire.

THE CO-HOST

Americans never seem to outgrow their need for cheerleaders and game show co-hosts are living proof of this. If you want to be a game show co-host, there's just no way around the fact that you have to be good-looking and possess a smile that would fuse plutonium. The job is not as easy and superficial as it may seem. After all, you must be able to:

1. read the entire alphabet both backwards and forwards.

2. demonstrate all the features of a modern appliance using only the parts of your body that don't talk.

3. put up with the host.

THE REGULAR GUEST

To be a regular guest on a game show is not just one of the most lucrative plums in show business, it's one of the more gratifying experiences a human can have. Just think of it, unless you're Nipsey Russell, and actually go to the trouble of writing little quips and poems, all you have to do is show up every day and say things you'd normally say and people will scream, cheer and send letters proposing marriage.

Seriously, you don't even have to get the answers to the questions right, which brings us to another point. As a game show regular, you will typically find yourself sitting opposite some schmuck who desperately wants to win money. Remember, that's not important. What's important is increasing your exposure. So if you have to choose between giving a glib answer that'll make millions of people chuckle and adore you or a correct answer, which will help the contestant win the money he needs to get his daughter a leg brace, guess which one the producers of the show, your agent and fans want you to give?

CELEBRITY HOMEWORK: Practice sitting in a box with your name on it. Make silly faces. Have someone ask you stupid questions. Give stupid answers.

Channeling: How To Be A TV News Celeb

One of the wonderful things about being an American is that there are no less than nine hundred TV stations you can tune into and vegetate in front of. Not only does this present American viewers with an extraordinary freedom of choice, it has also created a virtual boom in the celebrity business since every one of these stations has at least one anchorperson, a sports reporter and a weather person, as well as assorted in-depth reporters, movie critics, guest commentators and various other video flotsam and jetsam.

In fact, the only reason your beaming face isn't being beamed into your neighbors' homes at some point in the next twenty-four hours is that you're just not trying. Seriously, the real question isn't whether you can be a TV celebrity, the question is what kind you should become. (In this regard, a few words of caution are in order. Avoid doing a Sunday morning public service show—not even your grandmother will get up to watch. Also, don't host a local amateur hour. It's every bit as degrading to host one as it is to be a contestant.)

All things considered, the best kind of show to be on is the news. Just think, you don't even have to make things up! All you have to do is tell people what happened today or what you think might happen tomorrow, which is probably something you do already.

On a news show, the best thing to be is the weatherperson. You see, if you're the anchorperson, people will assume you're just an egotistical know-it-all who likes to wear make-up. If you do sports, they'll dismiss you as the kind of nerd who was the waterboy for his high school football team. But if you're the weatherperson, they'll like you for the simple reason that your forecasts will be wrong most of the time and being wrong most of the time is a quality most people admire in someone else.

CELEBRITY HOMEWORK:
TV NEWS ANCHORPERSON

1. Practice looking intelligent while reading something you don't understand.

2. Practice looking concerned while reading something you don't care about.

TV SPORTS REPORTER

Practice holding a microphone in front of something big and dumb (a cow, for instance).

TV WEATHERPERSON

Practice standing in front of a map that really isn't there.

Lip Service: How To Be A Celebrity Talk Show Host

Being a talk show host means you have reached the apogee of celebrityhood, and there's no further you can go until you can afford to retire and just be famous for doing nothing except playing in pro-am golf tournaments. Formerly, of course, there used to be only one kind of TV talk show, the late-night funny kind. These days there are various sorts, including the sensitive kind and the sociopathic kind. The fundamental rule to observe as host of any of these shows is to make sure a minimum of two lips are moving at all times. Each type of show, however, has its own set of rules.

HOW TO HOST A FUNNY TALK SHOW

Make fun of the band, Cleveland, the network, last night's audience or the fact that tonight's audience didn't laugh at your last joke. When desperate for a laugh, go for the groin. A simple reference to the breasts, crotch, toilet facilities or any well-known bodily function will also do in a pinch.

HOW TO HOST A SENSITIVE TALK SHOW

Talk about how difficult it is to be (a) a woman (b) a minority member (c) an addictive personality and how terrible it is that most men still refuse to share (a) their feelings (b) their paychecks (c) the rest of their lives. When you're desperate for a reaction, go for the heart strings.

HOW TO HOST A SOCIOPATHIC TALK SHOW

Talk about how our society would be a lot better off with more (a) women (b) minorities (c) addicted personalities. When you're desperate for a reaction, go for the throat.

HOW TO BE A TALK SHOW GUEST

Since you won't be required to talk about anything other than yourself, you'll probably find that even your first appearance on a talk show will be easy and enjoyable. There are, however, two rules to observe.

1. As soon as you sit down, mention a city, any city. At least 50 people will applaud and, for some inexplicable reason, the rest of the audience will seem to like you.

2. Before the show's over, make sure you mention that your family is more important to you than your career.

Keep in mind, however, that it's not all play

and no work. You're on a talk show for a serious reason—which is to sell your latest movie, book, record or whatever. Refuse to leave until the host has shown a clip from your movie, the jacket of your new album or the cover of your latest book to the national audience and never get so bogged down in discussing anything interesting that you neglect to mention your latest work at least once every other sentence. Remember, talk shows are really just hour-long commercials and the product is you.

CELEBRITY HOMEWORK: Put a desk and chair next to the living room couch, and sit there while talking to people. (If you want to be co-host, sit on the couch.)

The King And I: Royal Celebs

I f you want to be a celebrity, there is no easier way to do it than to be born into a royal family. Let's face it, if you can say something like, "Gee, I'd like to go to your party, but first I've got to check it out with my mom, thc Queen," you've got it made when it comes to getting your picture in the tabloids. If you're a royal, of course, talent is utterly beside the point and, as Prince Charles has confessed, intelligence can be an absolute handicap. All you really have to be able to do is nod, wave and occasionally wear thirty-seven pounds of clothes, which would seem not to eliminate anyone from contention, including junkie drag queens.

Sadly, few of us seem to be getting born into royalty these days; and if there's anything harder than getting born into a royal family, it's trying to marry into one. Before you can even curtsy and say, "Yes, your majesty," someone will have discovered your father was a Nazi plumber, and you'll be out on your ear. Solace may be taken, however, from the fact that all evidence suggests being a member of a royal family isn't really everything it's cracked up to be. After all, would you really want to go to bed with a guy who had ears like Prince Charles just for the opportunity to crack a bottle of champagne on the front of a submarine?

As members of a royal family, men who are actually homelier than their horses have no trouble getting on TV.

Painting By The Numbers: Celebrity Artists

There are about 200 million people who can draw, paint and sculpt, so if you want to be a famous artist, don't expect to be appreciated for your art. You see, what you need is not the ability to draw a puppy, pony or peony. What you need is an attitude. To succeed as a contemporary artist, observe the following fundamental principles.

1. BE ANGRY. Antagonize critics and art dealers and be generally disagreeable to everyone else. Contrary to what you may think, people will not resent this. In fact, once you become notorious as an angry artist, people will actually feel slighted if you go to a gallery opening and don't spit on their pants.

2. OBSERVE THE PRINCIPLE OF PERVERSITY. This means that at any social function, or whenever in public, you should do the exact opposite of what everyone else is doing. If everyone is having a good time, be miserable; if everyone's miserable, start laughing. Eventually you'll be recognized as a genius and can raise your prices.

3. LOOK HUNGRY. People still think starving artists are the best, so always tell people your work means more to you than food. Since most people are incapable of conceiving of anything more important than what's for breakfast, lunch or dinner, they'll be forced to conclude your work must be pretty significant. Of course, once you develop a reputation as a starving artist, you'll be invited to more cocktail parties, dinners and receptions than you could possibly attend; soon you'll have big, puffy cheeks and your pants won't fit. Not to worry, people will just assume your work is a commercial success.

4. OBEY THE LAW OF OBSCURITY. If you want to avoid total obscurity, make sure anything you say is totally obscure. Since you're an artist, people will assume you've probably said something deep, and they just don't get it.

CELEBRITY HOMEWORK: Practice the principle of perversity. Go to a funeral and laugh; go to a party and cry.

Strange Bedfellows: A Few Words On Political Celebrities

If you're not one of the Kennedys, it's probably not worth the effort. Politics is still fundamentally dull and drab, and you're going to find yourself making a lot of speeches to Kiwanis, senior citizens and other groups at the bottom of the glamour scale. There are, however, some reasons you may want to consider becoming a political celeb. For one thing, politics is one area in which someone who is ugly, fat and dumpy can not only be accepted, but actually excel. For another thing, it's one of the few places in our culture in which age still works to your advantage, so if you're wrinkled, wizened and generally too shrivelled to consider auditioning for a part in a major motion picture, perhaps politics is for you.

At any rate, the following test will give you some idea if you've got what it takes.

1. You associate the word "Russian" with
   (a) salad dressing.
   (b) a nation of Satan-worshipping anti-Christs.

2. Something everyone should know how to stuff is
   (a) a turkey.
   (b) a ballot box.

3. Your favorite song is
   (a) anything except "b."
   (b) "Happy Days Are Here Again."

4. Given your choice, you would rather watch
   (a) the motion picture of the year.
   (b) a poll.

Clearly, if you answered "b" to any of these questions, you were born to be a political celebrity. In fact, it would be hard to imagine your becoming a celebrity of any other sort. But don't worry, it's not hard. All you have to do is dress like a funeral director, learn to read from a teleprompter and form an opinion.* Then, after your first term, you can begin to ignore the drips, dregs and drones who elected you and start hobnobbing with megastars who have wearied of simply being wealthy and famous and would now like to change the world.

CELEBRITY HOMEWORK: Form an opinion. Investigate your parents.

---

* *It'll give the voters something to think about and give you something to fall back on when you're questioned by the press. All things considered, two opinions are probably one more than you'll need.*

If you're not a Kennedy, becoming a political celebrity may not be worth the effort.

Smile When You Say That: Beauty Contest Celebs

In all honesty, beauty pageants are really comedy shows, and the only people who seem not to know this are the contestants and their parents. Let's face it, even the Miss America pageant exists only so that people around the world will have something to snicker and sneer at one dull weekend in September.

The tragic part of the whole affair is that, after exposing their body parts and lack of talent to billions of people around the world, the losers will be instantly forgotten while the winners will have to spend the rest of their lives proving they aren't incorrigible airheads. Nonetheless, some women seem to be driven to parading around in bathing suits, presenting their buttocks to large crowds and smiling until they get earaches.

If you're one, here are a few dos and don'ts.

1. YOU CAN'T BE SERIOUS. Don't perform classical music, a modern dance piece or Shakespearean soliloquies, unless you can do it standing on your head while keeping beachballs in the air with your feet.

2. DON'T COME FROM MASSACHUSETTS. When was the last time Miss Massachusetts didn't look like one of the founding fathers? If possible, try to come from Texas or California. If you're from northern

California, remember to shave your armpits.

3. DON'T PLAY THE CLARINET. In living rooms around the world, this will inevitably prompt every crude, smirking, sexual innuendo imaginable. This is not an act the judges will reward or wish to see repeated. You will never make the final eight.

Beauty contests are really comedy shows.

So Proud You Could Bust: How To Be A Centerfold

There is no greater indication of the importance celebrityhood and notoriety have attained in our society than the fact that many parents now profess unabashed pride when their daughters appear nude in *Penthouse*, *Hustler* and *Playboy*. Despite the fact that many of these parents express the sentiment, "God gave my daughter a beautiful body, why shouldn't she show it off?" there are, unfortunately, some fuddyduddies who would rather not have their daughter's naughty bits examined in minute detail by a few million acne-plagued males. This type of closed-minded parent shamefully deprives his or her child of what is probably her only opportunity to become even a little famous.

If your parents are among this reluctant minority, you may find the following arguments useful in persuading them.

1. IT'S OKAY. It's nothing my gynecologist hasn't seen, and he's a doctor.

2. NUDITY IS NATURAL. Especially when you're wearing spike heels, a feather boa and a garter belt.

3. IT'S NOT REALLY PORNO OR ANYTHING. Seriously, the German shepherd was just there for protection.

NO NUDES IS GOOD NUDES

Okay, say you get your first exposure by exposing yourself for some, uhhhh, revealing pictures. Then later your career mushrooms, or you become Miss America or something, and the pictures are published. Confronted with this situation, the best thing to do is to declare that the photos are art or, at least, "tastefully done."

No matter how much wishful thinking you do, some nude pictures are clearly neither art nor tasteful, in which case you should do the following.

1. ISSUE A TEARFUL DENIAL. Swear the person in the pictures isn't you, even though she seems to have the same birthmarks, face and tattoos.

2. ISSUE A TEARFUL REGRET. Okay, so maybe it is you. But at the time the pictures were taken, you were so hungry you didn't realize your pants weren't on.

3. PUT TOGETHER A VEGAS ACT. It doesn't matter whether you can sing, dance or walk across a stage without falling into the orchestra pit, people will show up just to see if you'll take your pants off again.

CELEBRITY HOMEWORK: Practice smiling during your next gynecological examination.

The Write Stuff: Celebrity Authors

The fact that *TV Guide* is now one of our country's most popular magazine provides some clue to the esteem in which our culture holds the written word. Nonetheless, there are some people, who can't sing or dance and don't photograph well, who may actually wish to consider writing as a career. In all honesty, however, if more than twelve people ever buy anything you write, it's not going to be because they admire a nifty prose style, it's because (a) reading books is the only way they can get to sleep or (b) you've created some sort of public disturbance.

In regard to "b," maybe you should consider committing murder, or at least adultery, before you commit anything to paper. And if you can't stand blood, or the thought of alimony payments, you can always fall back on one of these tried and true literary conventions.

1. INSULT A MAJOR RELIGION. Islam would do nicely.

2. DECLARE YOURSELF A GENIUS. Hey, it worked for Oscar Wilde, Gertrude Stein, Steve Allen and John Steinbeck.

3. INSULT A MAJOR AUTHOR. Gore Vidal would work.

In any event, before you start pecking away in the attic writing something that may be noted with pleasure in the *New York Times* and ignored by everyone else, make sure you have something stimulating, fresh and important to say. Not in print either, you ninny, on talk shows.

Oscar Wilde, Gertrude Stein, John Steinbeck and Steve Allen haven't been afraid to declare themselves geniuses. Maybe you're one, too.

If I Only Had A Brain: Celebrity Models

In its own weird way, being a fashion model is one of the truly unique and wonderful forms of celebrityhood. As a model, you can become rich, famous and admired by millions just for wearing clothes—something most people on the planet manage to do with scarcely a second thought. As anyone in the fashion business will tell you, however, the competition to become a top model is dauntingly fierce. This is because it's the only way a person, whose talent consists largely of an ability to walk upright, can make a lot of money and become an object of public adulation, and that hardly excludes any of us. Nonetheless, if your only hope of becoming a celebrity is to become a mannequin, don't be a dummy. Follow the rules.

1. NEVER SAY ANYTHING INTELLIGENT. It would disappoint your fans, who just wouldn't understand. Literally.

2. WHEN YOU TALK, TALK ABOUT FOOD. One of the great things about being a model is that you never even have to open your mouth, unless you're going to spit out your gum. If you ever go on a talk show, insist that either (a) you have to diet all the time to keep your wonderful figure or (b) you can eat all you want and still keep your wonderful figure. At

any rate, if you discuss anything more profound than what you generally have for dinner, you'll be violating Rule Number One and can expect to get a lot of mail from confused and angry fans.

3. LEARN TO WALK UPRIGHT. It's really the sine qua non of the job. Once you learn to do it well, practice doing it without falling off a runway.

CELEBRITY HOMEWORK: No assignment. Tonight. Or ever.

HOW TO BE A CELEBRITY FASHION DESIGNER

Undoubtedly you've noticed the proliferation of celebrity fashion designers in the last ten years. Around the world, their names have spread like some sort of gluteal influenza. That's because, aside from the willingness to see one's name plastered on rumps around the world, it takes almost nothing to become a celebrity fashion designer. Clearly, humans have had two arms, two legs and a single head for billions of years now, and we all know that there are only four or five fundamental looks which are dusted off and proclaimed "radically new and different" once every four or five years on a sort of rotating schedule. As a fashion designer, therefore, your true mission in life is not to come up with some innovative way of festooning the human form, but rather to make a name for yourself. Once you've made a name for yourself, simply stick it on everything from pantyhose to pillow cases and you can make a fortune for yourself.

The Big Bucks: Celebrity Jocks

S adly, you can't fake hitting a 90 mph fast-ball, lifting 800 pounds or doing a one-and-a-half gainer with a full twist, which is really a shame, since there are a lot of people without much athletic talent who would like to be famous sports celebrities. If you have any ability at all, however, it's fairly easy to become a celebrity jock, since most of your cohorts will suffer from severe verbal handicaps. In fact, if you can manage to say something other than, "They played real good," you'll be recognized as a wit and quipster and be well on your way to becoming a legend. If you're a jock without much athletic talent, and find you can't usually manage to think of anything clever to say until about two days after the game, you'll soon discover nobody's even going to think about naming a candy bar after you, unless you become one of the "colorful characters" of your sport. Becoming a "colorful character" means you'll have to snap your teammates with a towel in the shower, spit beer on them from hotel balconies and generally engage in the sort of semi-demented behavior most people don't consider or tolerate once they're out of junior high. No matter how inane this seems, remember, you're going to write your autobiography someday, and you'll need something to talk about other than muscle tears and groin pulls.

Probably the most important thing in establishing yourself as a sports celebrity, though, is a good nickname.* Just make sure it lends itself to the sort of simple rhymes that can be easily chanted by a vast throng of drunks. And even if you're a woman,** make sure it has the manly stench of testosterone about it, something like "The Bull," "The Babe" or "The Hulk."

CELEBRITY HOMEWORK: Ask your parents or employer for a $400,000.00 increase in allowance/raise. Go to a bar and get in a fight.

---

* *Perhaps the best proof of the power of a good nickname may be seen in professional wrestlers. Without nicknames they'd just be fat showoffs who don't mind dressing in drag.*

** *or a reasonable facsimile*

**Without a good nickname, no one will care
how many home runs you hit.**

Hairstyles Of The Rich And Famous: How To Be A Rock Star

Everyone who has ever been a teenager in America has the right and, perhaps, obligation to release at least one long-playing album during his/her lifetime, so there are a lot of you who should pay close attention. Since you'll be trying to impress adolescents, remember neatness doesn't count. Neither will subtlety, irony or classical allusions. Rudeness, does, however. In fact, to determine if you have what it takes to be a rock star, just answer this simple question:

In your opinion, every teacher in America deserves to be (a) better paid or (b) tied to a stake in the desert and eaten by army ants.

Obviously, the answer is "b." The basic point to remember is that you should be able to convince kids you hate teachers just as much as they do, and if you had your way, all schools would be turned into head shops. Speaking of head, the other thing to bear in mind is that you're going to have to do some unusual things with that top of yours. (Need we mention Elvis, the Beatles, Bob Marley, Grace Jones or David Bowie?) Clearly, a distinctive coif is every bit as important as being able to deliver a ditty. Due to the limited number of things one can physically do to the top of one's skull, genuine originality is probably more difficult to achieve. Just remember to do whatever it is you're going to do in a hurry. Because in this field, if at first you don't succeed, you probably never will.

CELEBRITY HOMEWORK: Refuse to take out the trash. Mess up your room. Ask your parents for more allowance. Buy a guitar; don't worry about learning to play.

To succeed in the rock field, you've got to use what's between your ears. Your hair.

Going Full Bore: How To Be A PBS Celeb

There's a certain sort of person who desperately wants to be noticed but doesn't want to be soiled by an open association with the popular media. This is something of a quandary but not absolutely irresolvable. It just means you'll have to be a celebrity on PBS where no one will see you. Here are the rules.

1. DRESS LIKE YOUR PARENTS. Unless your parents are Cindy Lauper, Bob Guccione or Mr. T. But odds are that you live in Boston, so you probably dress like your parents anyway.

2. USE BIG WORDS. Don't worry if you don't understand them, no one else will either. Take William F. Buckley, for example. No one's really understood what he's been talking about for years, including himself.

3. DON'T SHOW YOUR GUMS. And don't snicker, sneer, snort or smile. After all, things are serious.

4. DON'T PANDER TO THE AUDIENCE. On PBS, you don't want to be a smarmy, sickening sycophant* like Regis or Merv. This shouldn't be much of a problem since there'll hardly ever be an audience.

---

* *See rule #2.*

If At First You Don't Succeed—Or At Any Point Thereafter

THE NEXT TO LAST RESORT: BE A BOXHEAD

If every other effort to make yourself a celebrity fails, there's still one option and that's to become a beefy baron of industry and paste your name and picture on hotels, airplanes or boxes of whatever it is you make. Don't laugh. It's not like it hasn't worked for Frank Purdue, Colonel Sanders, Mrs. Fields, Donald Trump and Leona Helmsley. And if your company doesn't own hotels or put stuff in boxes, just put yourself in the commercials like Lee Iacocca.

ABSOLUTELY THE LAST RESORT: PODIATRIST TO THE STARS

Okay, let's say you're a desperate bottom-of-the-barrel bore who has, since birth, been greeted with yawns and averted glances. All is not lost if you can simply make yourself useful to people who already are celebs. If, for instance, you become known as the "Podiatrist to the Stars," "CPA to the Stars," "Dentist to the Stars," or whatever, there's a chance you'll find yourself in *People* magazine as much as the celebs whose taxes you do, teeth you drill and corns you remove—and then you'll be one yourself.

Many successful business people have made themselves big celebrities by becoming boxheads.

Part II

THE BIZ

There's No Business Like Show Business,
But Is That All Bad?

How Much Talent Do You Need?

This question, quite naturally, occurs to a lot of young, aspiring celebrities, although not to anyone who's seen Raquel Welch act. The answer, of course, is that you need absolutely no recognizable talent whatsoever to be a highly acclaimed and respected celebrity. In fact, the time you spend developing and honing any talent you possess can actually impede your success by interfering with your ability to appear on talk shows and Barbara Walters specials. Besides, if talent were the least bit necessary to the attainment of celebrityhood, why is almost everyone in the entire world familiar with Bruce Willis?

ORIGINALITY: A SIN?

Another question asked by many young celebs concerns originality. Is it really necessary? Clearly, Madonna is living proof that originality is neither necessary nor particularly desirable. As every show biz mogul knows, most people find true originality unsettling, confusing and annoying. That's why sequels are so popular. That's why pop stars can go on imitating Marilyn Monroe and James Dean ad infinitum, not to mention ad nauseam. So don't worry about being an original. Just make sure you imitate the right person at the right time.

Certain Death

Unless you have a passionate craving for obscurity, there are certain fields you should avoid. Take poetry, for instance. It requires a lot of work and arouses an almost instant sensation of tedium in well over 99% of the public. Since Dylan Thomas died, the only poet who's become a celebrity is Nipsey Russell, and one Nipsey Russell is probably enough. The following are fields you should probably eschew.

1. MIME. Most people would rather assault a mime than watch one.

2. MODERN DANCE. All that pain! And who cares?

3. SHAKESPEAREAN ACTOR. All those words! And who cares?

4. CIRCUS CLOWN. You'll frighten children and revolt adults. This is fame?!

5. SITAR PLAYER. Perhaps one person in ten can differentiate between Indian music and a splitting headache.

Behind Every Successful Celebrity: A Guy With A Smelly Cigar

In your youth, you may come to the conclusion that you are blessed with beauty and/or talent. For a long time, you may even think that your beauty and/or talent will be sufficient to make you a huge show biz megastar. If you labor under this impression, forget it. The simple truth is that the real players in the celebrity game are not the actors, singers, violinists, what-have-yous. The real players are the agents and PR people. With them, you could be a star; without them, you're a nobody. Take Jayne Mansfield, for example. Though never possessed of any discernible talent other than her obvious ability to keep a tiger-skin bathing suit from falling to the ground, once a year her PR man would announce that she was marooned on a desert island and, within a week, every young male in the nation, galvanized by the thought that he might never see those jumbo funbags again, would go see one of her stupid movies. Now that, my friends, is talent. Moreover, the simple truth of the matter is that the agents, lawyers and PR people are the ones who make the money. And while celebrities may be the ones with household names, their agents are the ones with the big houses.

To see if you've got what it takes, take the following test.

1. A cover charge is
   (a) what you pay to get into a nightclub
   (b) what you pay to get somebody on the front of a magazine.

2. If you saw someone about to jump off a building, you would
   (a) talk him out of it
   (b) sell tickets.

3. A person with a truly inquiring mind is someone who
   (a) knows all about the arts and sciences
   (b) believes what they read in the *National Enquirer*.

If you answered "b" to any of the preceding questions, you've got the stuff. Now all you need are a small office and a cigar the size of somebody's forearm. Beautiful!

How Sharper Than A Serpent's Tooth: The Critics

When it comes to critics, celebs are caught in an excruciating bind. On one hand, every celeb wants critical approval almost as much as he wants his next breath. On the other, if the critics like you, almost no one else will. (Let's face it, calling something a "critical success" is just another way of telling the American public it can expect to fall asleep.)

Being shrewd, if not necessarily intelligent, most celebs choose to ignore the critics and pander to the popular taste. This does not mean, however, that as a celebrity, you will not be hurt by the witty barbs and nasty brickbats the critics will inevitably throw your way. Here are some things you should keep in mind to ease the pain.

1. In his best year, a critic will make less than 1% of what you make in your worst.

2. A critic has to sit and type all day on a chair that doesn't even have his name on the back.

3. In high school, critics were on the debating team and had severe acne while you were a cheerleader with a perfect complexion. Basically, they still hate you for this.

Okay, now don't you feel better about being called "an atavistic lump of mediocrity who doesn't have the talent required to portray a petunia in a seventh-grade play"? Good.

CELEBRITY HOMEWORK: Practice smiling bravely. Practice saying "I don't care what critics think; I only care what the public thinks."

In high school, critics were on the debating team while you were a cheerleader. They still hate you for this.

What's In A Name?

A rose may be a rose may be a rose, but a Rosencrantz is rarely a star. The sad truth is that most of us are not born with celebrity names, and if you've got an ethnic name, you're probably going to have to make it more blandly palatable. But don't feel badly, some of our biggest stars have had their names changed. Cary Grant, for instance, used to be Archibald Leach and Judy Garland's original name was so ridiculous nobody even wants to remember it. However, if you're really attached to the name your parents gave you, at least try to give it an unusual spelling, like Liza with a "z."

Then there's the issue of autographs. One school of thought says you should give one to every dink who asks for it because, after all, where would you be without your fans? The other says signing autographs will give you hand cramps, chip your nails and you'll never get to finish a meal in a public restaurant. And where would you be without food?

CELEBRITY HOMEWORK: Along with their noses, most celebs have not hesitated to dump their original names. These examples may prove useful in helping you devise your own celebrity moniker.

Original Name	Celebrity Name
Greta Louise Gustafssen	Greta Garbo

Original Name	Celebrity Name
Ramon Estevez	Martin Sheen
Tula Ellice Finklea	Cyd Charisse
Maurice Micklewhite	Michael Caine

What The World Needs Now

It's not love, sweet love, either. It's something to talk about. So if you want to move out of your parents' apartment and join the ranks of international superstars, it can't hurt to have some kind of attention-getting gimmick. Don't worry, it doesn't have to be anything particularly brilliant. Take Michael Jackson's* single white glove. Every winter millions of school children wander home in exactly the same state of deshabille without once having it reported on TV. Nonetheless, it was a coup. One night he wore a single glove and the next day, the entire world was talking about it. See how easy it can be? What's next? Socks that don't match? Wearing half a brassiere?

Another way to keep tongues wagging, of course, is to keep folks wondering about your sexual proclivities. The master of this was, indisputably, Liberace.** In addition to his ability to create and exploit show biz's most shamelessly spectacular gimmicks, the man was able to enhance his career and increase his fortune by encouraging relentless public speculation about whether the stunning, young men he was seen with were just there to carry his luggage. Anyway, if anybody ever starts wondering if you're gay, don't sweat it. This could be the boost your career needs.

---

*   *the black Liberace*

**   *the original, white one*

Who knows what the great gimmick will be?

How To Be Beloved

As a celebrity you will find yourself in a precarious position. On one hand, you occupy a position of power and prestige. On the other hand, it could all be over at any second, and you could find yourself playing the lead in "The Flower Drum Song" at a theatrical supper club outside Sioux City. Despite what many people think, the trick to maintaining a high popularity rating does not lie in maintaining high artistic standards. After all, look at Orson Welles. Despite his insistence on quality, he remained little more than a blackballed ball of fat relegated to buffoonish appearances on late-night talk shows. On the other hand, there is Bob Hope. Having made scant claim to talent, he has nonetheless rolled merrily along singing his irritating theme song all the way to the bank for decades. The comparison is instructive for it demonstrates what you must do to survive as a celeb, which is simply to seem sincere, flatter your audiences and appear humble. Specifically:

1. ALWAYS SAY HOW GLAD YOU ARE TO BE WHEREVER YOU ARE. Remember, the audience has to live there; tomorrow, you'll be back in Beverly Hills.

2. ALWAYS SAY YOUR FAMILY COMES FIRST. Try not to laugh.

3. INSIST THAT YOU WOULD STILL BE DOING WHAT YOU DO EVEN IF

YOU DIDN'T MAKE A CENT. Again, try not to laugh.

4. WAVE THE FLAG. You don't have to be for or against any government policies. Just say America is the greatest country on earth, and anyone who burns the flag should be burnt at the stake. Everyone will go home happy.

YOUR HATING RATING

No matter how hard they try, some celebrities find it hard to be beloved. If you're one of these, you may find it reassuring that, even though the public doesn't like you, there are still millions of people all over America who count on you. No, no, they aren't counting on you to deliver a good song, a snappy joke or a sterling performance. They're simply depending on you to show up with some regularity on TV and in print, so they can sit there glowering and cursing and, eventually, rid themselves of the accumulated venom, spleen and malice that festers in all of us. Much like the sacrificial lambs and oxen of other cultures, you see, some celebs perform the important function of giving the public someone on whom it can focus every last, little nasty sentiment and leave it feeling, individually and collectively, cleansed. That's why every year certain programs which invariably evoke the response, "I can't believe this show is on again," are on again. That's why certain people who lack any indication of talent are seen with enormous regularity and have simply spectacular ratings. Yes! It's all because our ability to focus our loathing on these people helps prevent wars, stop spousal beatings and mitigates our overwhelming desire to kick the cat. So remember, the next time you find yourself warbling a song off-key or telling a joke that doesn't make anybody laugh, you're not just humiliating yourself, you're practically performing a public service.

Just because people don't like you, doesn't mean they don't want you around.

How To Be Absolutely, 100% Sincere

Sincerity does not come easily to many of those who want to be celebrities. Nonetheless, the appearance of sincerity is at times an absolute prerequisite for the proper performance of the job.

Since the appearance of sincerity may be the single most difficult skill for you to master, I recommend that you work at it. Hard. Every morning, you should practice a sincere facial expression for at least fifteen minutes while looking in the mirror. (There, that's not so bad, is it?) If you have difficulty determining what a sincere expression looks like, remember dogs do it well, so go look at one and try to imitate it.

CELEBRITY HOMEWORK: Once you have mastered a sincere facial expression, practice combining it with the following phrases.

1. my oldest and dearest friend

2. one of my favorite people

3. I'd like to share this feeling with you.

As a celebrity, there's probably a lot about sincerity you can learn from a dog.

A Few Words About Awards

Of course, awards mean nothing to you, but they mean a lot to your parents, your producers and everyone else who worked so hard just to give you this opportunity to stand in front of a national television audience and talk about yourself, so be sure to take your time and thank virtually every person you've ever met. Who knows, the people in the viewing audience may even think it's because you're modestly trying to share the credit and not just because it'll let you hog the limelight for an extra minute or two. And don't worry about those people who will complain that your speech was vain, repetitious and boring. If they were in your glittering pumps, they'd be right out there thanking their fifth-grade gym teacher and the nice people who lived down the street when they were kids.

However, if you're already a megaceleb, remember that you'll get the most publicity by NOT accepting an award. So if it's obviously your year to get an Oscar or an Obie, announce weeks in advance that you will refuse to accept the award, attend the event or even, henceforth, acknowledge its existence. Finally, if you're a megaceleb who's already refused to show up and accept an award on a number of occasions, it may be time for you to appear and make a big stink about something that has nothing to do with show biz. For instance, animal rights. Spill gerbil blood on the podium or pull out pictures of tortured monkeys. Without question, people will remember this long after they've forgotten who won the Oscar.

CELEBRITY HOMEWORK: Make a list of every person you've ever known in your life. (Don't forget to include God.) Practice repeating this list in front of people who are asleep.

Charity And The Celebrity

Few things are as dear to the heart of the average celebrity as his favorite charity. This is largely because nothing else could even vaguely promise to give him twenty-four hours of gloriously uninterrupted exposure on national TV. In short, a telethon. Imagine nothing but *you, you, you* on almost every television from coast to coast for one full day!

There are a couple of things to remember, however. One is that you're going to have to look ultra-sincere most of the time, and that may not be easy for you, so knuckle down and practice. (See chapter on "How to Be Absolutely, 100% Sincere.") Also remember that you must use infinite care when selecting the organization upon which you intend to shower your attention and generosity. Pick the right one, and you'll be a household name. Pick the wrong one, and you could end up with a picture of yourself next to a dead dog in a black and white brochure.

At any rate, there are two things you have to remember to do a telethon.

1. LOOK GOOD AT THE BEGINNING.
   If you don't, people won't appreciate the wrenching, emotional experience you're about to endure; they'll just figure you're drunk.

2. LOOK LIKE HELL AT THE END. By the time you're through, victims of the cause should feel guilty you're forced to

go through this every year. The poster child should feel he owes you an apology. The audience should wonder if you've just had a nervous breakdown.

2 8 4 1 5 3 3 9

By the end of a telethon, the audience should feel more sympathy for you than for the victims of whatever cause you represent.

Retire Early, Retire Often

After you've been on top for a while, your career will inevitably begin a long, slow slide backwards. When you're introduced on a talk show, an almost audible boredom will drift through the air. In restaurants, people won't recognize you even when you sit right under your own caricature. At this point, friends will start to make gentle suggestions about a "graceful exit," and you may feel as though you'd have to light your hair on fire right in the middle of the Academy Award presentations to get the slightest bit of attention. But don't. Not right away. First, announce your retirement.

You see, to many celebs, announcing retirement plans serves the same function that going-out-of-business sales do for retail store owners: It boosts sales and assures them of going on practically forever. And no matter how many times you've "retired" before, there's no reason why, in the words of Ol' Blue Eyes, you can't do it "just one more time." Here's how.

1. Call a press conference and announce that this is the last time you'll do whatever it is you do in public.

2. Have a big, farewell performance.

3. Wait one year and repeat.

Like the unicorn, a graceful and permanent retirement from show biz has often been talked about but never actually seen.

OLD CELEBS DON'T FADE AWAY, THEY JUST DIE

The closest we can come to certifiable evidence that life everlasting actually exists is what has happened to Elvis, James Dean and Marilyn Monroe. If you're a real celebrity, your name will unquestionably live a lot longer than you. You can also expect to be admired more after your death than when you were here on earth annoying the public and irritating directors. Too bad you won't be here to accept the kudos.

Part III

"What rage for fame attends
            both great and small!
Better be damned than mentioned not at all."
                                        John Wolcot

You're Not
What You Eat—
You're Where You Eat

Next to a talk show or awards show, the restaurant is the most important place a celeb will appear. That's because this is where you will make connections with agents and producers and hobnob with other celebs, not one of whom will actually go to see your movie or play. This is also where the paparazzi are most likely to catch you in the act of being yourself, so dress nice, and maybe you'll end up in *People* magazine.

In a celeb bistro, of course, schmoozing is more important than eating, so don't just sit down and shovel food in your face. On your way to your table, you should wave to at least ten people and exchange huggies and air kissies with eight. After you're seated, try not to eat too much. For one thing, if your mouth's always full of food, it'll keep you from talking about yourself as much as you'd like. For another, look at what happened to Orson Welles.

Finally, never forget that a restaurant is never best judged by the quality of the food it puts on your plate, but rather by the number of pictures of you it puts on the wall.

CELEBRITY HOMEWORK: Ask a friend or relative to hold open the car door for you while you practice getting in and out.

Remember, your favorite restaurant won't necessarily be the one with the best food.

GILT BY ASSOCIATION

One of the cardinal rules of celebrityhood is to be seen with other celebrities, even if they don't particularly want you around. This simply means you should go to all the hot clubs and "in" restaurants, hang around and say hello to celebrities even though they won't know who you are and could care less. When you see celebs getting their pictures taken, you should simply step into the background, smile and give the photographer your name. Initially, of course, celebrities will boil with anger and resentment whenever you do this. As celebs become accustomed to seeing your name in photo captions next to theirs, however, they will come to resent your presence less, and ultimately you will become something of a celebrity yourself.

You're Not Always Where You Eat—Sometimes You're Where You Live

As a celebrity, you'll find the world is divided into three parts: Beverly Hills, Manhattan and Anywhere Else. From a celebrity perspective, of course, it really is pointless to live Anywhere Else and under no circumstances should you live in a trailer camp or some place that has mail delivered RFD. *There is one important exception to this rule, however:* If you're a writer or a star of the first magnitude, you can actually increase your fame and enhance your mystique by living Anywhere Else. If, for instance, you're a big film star and move to the boonies, you can be virtually assured a major publication will do a story on that semi-interesting fact once a year. Similarly, if you're a writer who announces his intention to become a recluse, you can count on having hordes of people spend their entire lives trying to figure out where you went. This means you'll be a cult figure and continue to be famous whether you ever write again or not.

No matter where your home is, it should have a pool that in some way reflects your personality and the way in which you achieved success. Liberace, for instance, had a pool shaped like a piano, while Jack Benny had one shaped like a violin. Brooke Shields, in all probability, has one with no deep end.

As a celeb, you'll want to live in a home that reflects your personality. As frequently as possible.

My Body, My Body, No Body Quite So True

In your quest to become a star, everything else in your life becomes disposable. This includes friends, relatives and, of course, your nose. Here are some of the alterations you may want to make to your body and a few simple tests to help you determine if they're necessary.

BODY PART	HOW TO TELL IF IT NEEDS WORK
NOSE	• Have you ever been told you looked like you were eating a banana when you weren't? • Have you ever been compared to a toucan or Barry Manilow?
STATURE	• Have you ever been told you looked like you were standing in a hole when you weren't? • Have you ever been compared to a a fire hydrant, Gary Coleman, Herve Villechaize or Michael J. Fox? • Since reaching the age of 20, have you ever had to sit on a telephone directory to see over the dashboard of your car?
EARS	• Have you ever been told you were holding potato chips next to your head when you weren't?

	• Have you ever been compared to Dumbo the Flying Elephant, Prince Charles or Mr. Spock?
	• If you run quickly into the wind, will your feet leave the ground?
TEETH	• Have you ever been asked not to smile in a group picture?
	• Have you ever been compared to a hyena, a picket fence or Mr. Ed?
	• When you smile at children, do they scream?

If you answered "yes" to any of the above questions, you probably need a few appropriate nips and tucks. Please note, however, that these days you don't have to have the perfect face and/or body to become a celebrity. In fact, having a peculiar, distinguishing feature can be an absolute boon to your career. Need I mention such noble precedents as Durante, Streisand, Terry Thomas and Fanny Brice? In short, you may be able to make a name for yourself just be being funny-looking. So maybe you don't have to change a thing.

CELEBRITY HOMEWORK: Look closely at your face in a mirror and figure out which is your best side, then take off all your clothes and decide which body parts have to go.

Being Loved
For Your Mind

Everyone who starts out being loved for the tilt of his nose or the shape of her body, ultimately wants to be admired for something more profound. Sadly, the deepest reflection most celebs have ever undertaken has involved a three-sided mirror and, in all honesty, few have spent the requisite time poring over musty books in lonely libraries increasing their intellectual capacities, having preferred to go to the beach instead. Worst of all, once the public has you pegged as a moron, it's almost impossible to change their thinking on the subject. No matter how many hours you log at the Actors' Studio or how resolutely you appear in public clutching a dog-eared copy of the collected works of Ibsen, when it comes to intellectual attainment, they're still likely to lump you together with dogs that can sing and bears that ride bikes. This being so, the important thing is to appear relatively smart right from the beginning. But don't despair, it's not like you have to know the atomic weight of plutonium or anything. In fact, there are relatively few things you need to know to convince nine out of ten Americans you're some kind of genius.

THINGS EVERY CELEBRITY SHOULD KNOW

The Arts

1. Shakespeare was a writer.

2. Rembrandt was a painter.

3. *Waiting for Godot* is your favorite play.

The Sciences

1. There are nine planets in the solar system, and the sun is in the middle.

2. All the dinosaurs died a long time ago.

3. Stalactites are the things that hang from the ceiling.

History

1. George Washington was the father of our country.

2. Lincoln freed the slaves.

3. Betsy Ross did the flag.

CELEBRITY HOMEWORK: Watch an episode of "Masterpiece Theater." Hide your comic books.

The Laws of Relativity

In America, there are more people who worship the family than God. So even though you've probably been married several times, haven't seen your children in years and might not recognize them if you did, you must always insist that *your family is the most important thing in your life*. Always follow this statement up by saying, with a straight face, that if you had to choose between your family and your career, you would give up your career.

There are, of course, other ways in which family ties may be useful. One is simple nepotism. The quickest, easiest and surest route to success is to be the child of a celeb. So if you're fortunate enough to have famous parents, make the most of them. No matter what you do, the media will make a big deal out of your first effort and at least five million people can be expected to see your first movie, listen to your first album or read your first book if only to figure out what kind of fool you intend to make of yourself.

Suppose, however, you have famous parents but find yourself so sadly deficient in talent that you couldn't even do a passable job of acting in a major motion picture. Does this mean you must resign yourself to becoming a butcher, a baker or a candlestick maker?! No way! Just write a vicious exposé about Mom and/or Dad, and within three months, you'll be on every talk show in the world. So go ahead. Tell the world Mommy used to wash your face with an eggbeater, and Daddy used to play hide the tamale with the Mexican maid. Of course, your parents may not like the revelations, but being celebs, you can be sure they'll appreciate the publicity.

Finally, let us suppose you aren't talented and your parents aren't famous. Your family can still help you achieve a certain sort of celebrity if you have what it takes to be a show biz mother. In fact, some of today's biggest celebs have gone straight from the womb to the commerical photographer's studio before their placentas were properly dry. Well, rather than carp and criticize, we say, "Hail, show biz moms!" Undaunted by the fact that their offspring have hardly begun to speak, let alone demonstrate an interest in landing a speaking part in Polanski's next big film, these women have forged ahead laying the foundations for their kids' careers.

Take this test to see if you have the mettle to join their ranks and become one of the few, the proud, the mama-rines!

1. You think of your child as
   (a) the fruit of your loins.
   (b) a major talent.

2. You would be most pleased if your child would take his/her first step
   (a) at home.
   (b) on a sound stage.

3. If a major director wanted your nine-year-old to appear in a semi-pornographic film, you would

naturally need to discuss this with
(a) her father.
(b) her agent.

Give yourself zero points for an "a" answer, five points for a "b." A score of ten points or more is an indication you're a real mother.

CELEBRITY HOMEWORK (children only): Make a list of all the rotten things your parents have ever done to you—include spankings and being sent to your room without dessert. Get an agent. Required reading: *Mommie Dearest.*

CELEBRITY HOMEWORK (mothers only): Sign your kid up for dance lessons, singing lessons, piano lessons and acting. Get an agent.

"M" is for the megastar she made me.

Your Entourage

As you become increasingly famous, you'll find yourself surrounded by a bunch of chuckleheads who will be known as your entourage. This means they'll try to mooch free tickets, meals and drinks from you every chance they get, and the rest of the time just hang around your pool.

If you're young and callow and not absolutely sure you have an entourage, here are a few ways you can identify someone who thinks he's in it.

1. Does this person laugh at your jokes before you finish them?

2. Has this person ever called you his "oldest and dearest friend" twice in one sentence?

3. During the course of a day is this person more likely to hug and kiss you than your spouse?

If the answer to any of the above questions is "yes," the person is either a member of your entourage or Regis Philbin and, in any event, you don't want him hanging around your house unless he promises to keep it clean.

As you might suspect, you've got to be very careful about having an entourage. While moving in this sort of herd can often get you a tabloid photographer's attention, and involves the kind of slavering adulation any celebrity adores, it can also be a major drain on your finances; and once your money's gone, you'll find your entourage has gone too, so why bother? But don't worry, like rodents, insects and other pests, an entourage is relatively easy to get rid of it you take the proper steps.

1. Drain the pool.

2. Refuse to pay for their drinks.

Within two weeks, people who formerly considered themselves to be members of your entourage will all be members of someone else's entourage and, mostly likely, have already forgotten they ever knew you.

CELEBRITY HOMEWORK: Pretend the other members of your family aren't related to you but just live in the same house because you're a star. Imagine the larger members of your family are bodyguards and instruct them to keep the smaller members of your family from bothering you.

Celebrity English

In the old days, you used to be able to buy a small egg or a small box of detergent. Now eggs arc "large," "extra large" or "jumbo," and detergent boxes are "family size," "king size" or "super king size." This serves to illustrate, as chicken farmers and soap manufacturers know, that in our culture, understatement gets you nowhere, particularly in show biz. For example, to be merely a "star" these days is to be a nobody. If you're anything less than a "megastar," you may as well be back in Kansas shucking corn. Beyond this, the basic rules of celebrity syntax are fairly simple.

1. Any sentence which does not contain the words "I," "me" or "mine" may not be grammatically correct.

2. Your name should always be first on the credits and the biggest on a marquee.

In addition you should be aware that there are certain words and phrases which, when used by a celebrity, may have a different import than they do in the context of an ordinary conversation. As in the following:

ORDINARY USAGE	CELEBRITY MEANING
"my oldest and dearest friend"	Refers to any other human being.

"a true genius"	Refers to any other human being and highly skilled animals, such as trained dogs and horses that can count.
"a blockbuster, a smash, a triumph or hit"	Refers to any recently released record, book or movie.
"a deeply humble man"	Refers to someone who would have to sit underneath his own portrait to be recognized.
"a critical success"	Refers to something boring.
"a popular success"	Refers to something stupid.
"I'm looking for the right script."	I am virtually unemployable.
"one of the truly sweet people in the business"	Refers to someone who has pictures of you fornicating with an animal.

CELEBRITY HOMEWORK: Write a story describing what you did last summer using all of the above phrases in the correct celebrity context.

True Confessions

Confession is good for the soul. It can also be good for your ratings. Say you haven't had a hit in years, and you find yourself being ignored by the media. Gulp, what to do?! One sure way back into the limelight is to admit to some horrible affliction of the soul, and check into a clinic for treatment. As soon as your agent releases the news that you're an alcoholic, on the edge of a nervous breakdown or a kitten molester, you'll find yourself surrounded by interviewers who can hardly wait to tell the world how wonderful and courageous you are. It's just that simple, and believe me, you'll never do an easier interview in your life. All you have to tell the media is (1) you've been bad (2) you're sorry and (3) you'll never do it again.

Before you know it, people will regard you as some sort of hero, and you'll have to hire extra staff just to sort your fan mail.

At This Time
My Client Would Like
To Announce That
He Wants To Be Alone

If you're like most celebs, you will spend years crying yourself to sleep because no one has ever heard of you outside of your immediate family and a couple of neighbors. During these years, you will do virtually anything to become famous. You will abandon your spouse and children, throw yourself—clothed or unclothed—in front of any camera and make extravagant promises to the Deity if only He will get you a guest spot on Oprah Winfrey.

Once you become famous, however, it's a whole new ballgame. Now you can actually get much more publicity by insisting that you never wanted to be famous* and would like everybody to go away and let you alone. At this point in your career, you will become known throughout the world for avoiding the press, attacking photographers and telling people you don't do interviews. In fact, if you ever permit an interview, it should only be so you can tell the interviewer how much you hate being interviewed.

CELEBRITY HOMEWORK: Go to your room and lock the door. Don't come out until every member of your family comes to ask what's wrong.

---

* *Because that's not what life's all about. What life's all about, remember, is your family.*

96

AFTER ALL, WHAT GOOD IS FAME AND FORTUNE IF YOU CAN'T MAKE OTHER PEOPLE HAPPY?

One of the great things about being a celebrity is that it gives you complete license to throw tantrums in public with little fear of reprisal. For instance, if someone wants to take your picture right there on the street, there's no reason in the world you can't just take his camera and smack him right across the bridge of the nose with it. And anytime you want, you can get waitresses fired, blackjack dealers canned and hat check girls put on permanent unemployment just because you're you and that's beautiful. And just think, if you ever get to be a megaceleb, you won't even have to beat up people yourself. You can hire people to do it for you.

CELEBRITY HOMEWORK: Hand somebody a camera, and ask him to take your picture. When the flash goes off, hit him over the head with it.

Celebrity Dressing

Clothes may or may not make the man. However, clothes often *are* the celebrity. Frequently, in fact, a celebrity's clothes will become, justifiably, more famous than the person wearing them. Typically, in cases in which a celebrity becomes known for his smart clothes, there is also the strong implication that the clothes are at least as smart as the celeb himself.

A related topic is the matter of going incognito. Many people assume the object of going incognito is to allow a celeb to go unrecognized in public and unmolested by the masses. This assumption is, of course, laughable. The whole point of going incognito is to establish the fact that you're so easily recognized, there's no way you can step out into the street without being pursued by paparazzi and mobbed by millions. To ensure this, many celebs adopt "trademark" disguises (i.e., Garbo's sunglasses and Jackie O's scarves) which make them more recognizable when they're incognito than when they aren't.

Why should Halloween come just once a year?

A Star Is Born And It's Wearing Your Shoes

Now that you know what it takes, it's time to get famous. Simply fill in the blanks below and, before you know it, you'll be hosting your own show. So what are you waiting for? Let's get started!

1. **Pick A Theme Song.** (Note: Avoid oriental music.)
   My theme song is _____ .

2. **Make Up A Discovery Story** (Note: Use twenty-five words or less.)
   How I was discovered.

   _____
   _____ .

3. **Pick A New Celebrity Name.** (See Chapter "What's in a Name.")
   My new name is _____ .

4. **Pick A Schtick.** (See Chapter "What the World Needs Now.")
   My new gimmick is _____ .

5. **Pick A Hairstyle.** My new celebrity hairstyle will make me look like ___ .

6. **Pick A Talent.** (Note: This is optional.)
   My new talent is _____ .

7. **Start A Fan Club.**
   The name of my new fan club is

   _____ .

   The president* of my new fan club is

   _____ .

   The P.O. Box of my new fan club is

   _____ .

*   *If currently without an agent, list friend, pet or relative.*

This book is published by

PRICE STERN SLOAN
Los Angeles

whose other riotous books include:

THE FIRST REALLY IMPORTANT
SURVEY OF AMERICAN HABITS

YOU'VE BEEN MARRIED TO LONG WHEN. . .

YOU KNOW YOU'RE DEPRESSED WHEN. . .

MURPHY'S LAW AND OTHER REASONS
WHY THINGS GO WRONG -
BOOKS ONE, TWO & THREE

and many, many more
These titles and others can be bought wherever
books are sold, or may be ordered directly
from the publisher.

PRICE STERN SLOAN
360 North La Cienega Boulevard, Los Angeles, CA 90048-1925